# Tracing Shadows

## Portrait Poems of People

*poems by*

# Itala Langmar

*Finishing Line Press*
Georgetown, Kentucky

# Tracing Shadows

## Portrait Poems of People

Publisher: Leah Maines

Editor: Christen Kincaid

Cover Design: Itala Langmar

Author Photo: James L. Merriner

Printed in the USA on acid-free paper.
Order online: www.finishinglinepress.com
also available on amazon.com

Author inquiries and mail orders:
Finishing Line Press
P. O. Box 1626
Georgetown, Kentucky 40324
U. S. A.

# Table of Contents

**Part One: Portraits of the Living**

## Part Two: Portraits from the Other Side

*Dedicated to James L. Merriner, without whose loving support and expert editing this book would never have seen the light.*

# Part One: Portraits of the Living

# Tracing Andre

My name is Andre.
Forty-three years old.
Out of work now.
I was a worker, moving boxes,
  painting walls, scrubbing basements,
  digging holes.
One weekend a friend called me
  with a skinny crooked tree
  he got for sale at Home Depot.
"Hey, Andre, could you dig me a hole
  for this tree, make it grow?"
 I dug a deep hole, put some
  unmentionable stuff in it.
Next spring, the tree was luscious.
I have the touch.
More people with trees to plant call me.
I dig and settle them in September.
Come May, the trees are glorious,
  fat and green, limbs embracing the sky.
I was a legend then, me and Elton John,
  my singer. I was Rocket Man then.
Now I am a retired planting tree man.
I got God in my heart, trying to get Him
  on my cell phone.
Sitting here against a wall,
  no place to go, to sleep tonight.
You could call me homeless. I see
  myself as rising star again soon.
Call myself a guy in search of a tree
  to be planted.
A guy in search of joy.

## Tracing Sherri

My name is Sherri.
This is mine for now:
   clouds at dusk
   never menacing
   willows in the wind.
Mine is the time for indulging
   a mental collection of postcards:
My child a white daisy
My husband a foundation
My closets harmonious
My future undisturbed.
All this is mine
   indefinite but not eternal
   rolling slowly on a trail
   of turquoise stones.

# Tracing Stan

My name is Stan.
I am accomplished in parenthood
  guiding my kids without push.
I walk with ease among elegant gardens
  ruminating about the painter Monet
  his lilies confused and remote.
My tastes are distinguished and rare:
  uncommon trees
  writers of value
  cars of impossible frames.
Colors intensely opaque, e.g.,
  marigold orange.
Check out the 1964 Karmann Ghia
  superb in Italian design.
I often sit on the fifth step of my home
  reflecting on why I detest
  movies in general and poetry also:
In my opinion poetry is useless,
  and I beg, if you dare,
  to be contradicted.

## Tracing Sharon Ph.

I am Sharon Ph.
A master perfection-seeker
   in thoughts and actions.
As a teacher I am severe, demanding,
   scrutinizing but encouraging.
I want the very same effort from my
   well-dressed, encyclopedic husband,
   a man slender and elegant.
I myself indulge in fashion,
   white flowing tunics by Eileen F., my choice.
I am happier when I love than when
   I am loved.
I adore my man mostly for his
   intransigence in moral convictions.
He would never abandon a sick me
   as did the devil married to Frida.
My kids and their kids please me.
They bring me yellow sticks they
   call roses.
My life is up mostly.
I am grateful for the rare days
   when I touch happiness
   with my palomino-colored toes.

# Tracing Glen

Good afternoon. I am Glen.
I trust in the tangible,
  in good manners,
  in the deductive Socratic way,
  inductive ones also.
I am by nature a leader,
  by training an educator.
For fun I guide liberal-minded people
  toward the appreciation of critical
  writings: the essays, the short stories,
  the editorials, often alarming, always
  engaging.
I have opinions on values,
  and provide evidential support,
  efforts my wife decrees worthwhile,
  beneficial.
The radiant one is often
  an improbable fan of mine.
I have affinities for possessions,
  pricey but none ostentatious.
A car is not just a car—it can be
  a movable sculpture.
A poem is not only a string
  of beautiful words
  but an exhortation to reflect,
  consider and select a design
  for a life more rewarding.
I explore themes of justice, loyalty,
  social issues, political issues,
  death.
I cherish the highlights of my life
  as one of God's children,
  sitting under the majestic tree
  with the trembling leaves.

# Tracing Kay

I am Kay, not really.
I am Kay Lynn
   so-called from the one intent on
   making me over as herself
   the oh-so-perfect daughter.
I am called brilliant now
   but the price was high,
   my soul dispirited
   a stranger to myself.
Some consolation?
A beautiful tree.
A tree that looks at God
   all day 'cause God alone
   can make a tree
   as the beloved poem says.
To me, uncertain, flippant me,
   the golden silk is real
   the silk of painting,
   the shining silk of Art Noveau,
   of Klimt is real.
The silk I roll in to get transmuted
   to get transformed, to be new
   to be the one I am in dreams,
   elegant, alluring with Tiffany
   shooting stars in my white tresses.
Mother would look at me again
   and again, contented.
Would she then smile?

## Tracing Milanne

Milanne is my name
There is definition in it
But I prefer Gigi
  a more fluid one
  unrelated to female lawyers
  corporation bosses
  Internet designers
  electrical engineers.
They talk in words precise,
  reverential, absurd.
Not me: words have color and feelings,
  they suggest mind reflections
  lost sunsets
  back-yard wildflowers
  back-porch whisperings . . .
I choose and recite words with
  vigilance, caressing them as
  invisible amulets.
I observe with dread
  the declining minds
  of our pathetic leaders
  the corrosion of intelligence
  of the million followers
  of Kim Something on Facebook.

Hey, God, my long-lost friend
  forever out of reach,
  are you doing anything for us
  wherever you are?

# Tracing Maria Vanessa

I am Maria Vanessa, stylist of fashion.
For my clothes I choose classic
   harmony and restraint.
A touch of Dali's inspired Schiapparelli,
   butterflies on my jacket's edges yes,
   but none of her bugs.
In the mirror I am gracious
   without the exalting felicity,
   the contentment of Degas' portraits.
I am afraid of being caught in
   the rain, the rain makes me tremble
   *mi da un tremore*, grief without
   reason, a *Verlainesque presagio*,
   short and intense.
I like written stories: other people's
   lives to consider and learn.
My mind likes to travel.
In summer I wear Ferretti organza
   dresses dragging their white lace
   on dusty streets. *Bella figura.*
I do not answer when
   people ask me where I am going.

# Tracing Casey

I am Casey the painter,
Very good at my trade
Famous for speeding
  with elegant moves
  from wall to white wall.
No mess, no mistakes,
  precision in mind.
The people who hire me are curious.
They want to know things about me.
I pay no attention.
I speak little.
I think to myself like Uncas,
  like Chingacook,
  my American heroes.
I pay no attention.
When done I jump in my truck,
  sorry, not the blazing black
  with gray stripes
  of my dreams
  not yet but soon.
And my girl in super-tight shorts
  and long golden hair
  will sit next to me, singing . . .
Life is good, God is everything.

## Tracing Nancy

My name is Nancy, retired teacher
  of bright adolescents.
Each one I loved like my own.
My job was to assist, expand,
  and enchant their minds
  in measured sequences.
I made them learn Napoleon, Pericles,
  heroes and villains, made them see
  weaknesses and strengths.
I used to tell them, study hard,
  read poetry, swing from tall trees,
  feed the birds.
About me: Now I walk in the park,
  never alone.
He is invisible, always
  walking in front of me.
I tell him I know you are
  who you say you are.
Walk slow, talk to me. I want to
  be with the Lord, your Father.
Does repentance work, even to
  seventy times seven?
When he turns and gives a silent smile
I feel a spaciousness in my center.
The birds are there, the lake, blue skies,
  with merciful breezes not yet severe . . .

# Tracing Paul

I am Paul, a lifelong lover of learning.
History, science, philosophy, ancient,
   theoretical, contemporary:
   I am talking string theory and memes.
Gravitational waves are OK,
   better for me before
   their discovery.
I was born curious, a skinny kid
   with selected *Encyclopedia*
   *Brittanica* volumes under my bed.
Now retired, I spend afternoons on the
   floor of my large living room with
   my dog, Gretchen, amid ponderous
   books.
Marcus Aurelius, Herodotus, Aristotle,
   St. Augustine, my unfailing, devoted
   companions.
No poets, I am sorry.
T. S. Eliot does not make it for me.
But O! the cryptic formulas of Albert
   the Genius!
Now those scribbles, my joy,
   keep my brain's molecules
   in a state of happy agitation.

## Tracing Susan

I am Susan, a woman of clarity,
  concision, competence.
My closets are organized,
  my basement sparse,
  my shoes in order of crescendo necessity,
  each pair with its complementary purse.
My front garden, pure joy, is
  non-Euclideanly perfect,
  a geometry of fluid low greens,
  gentle and rare with morning glory
  and impatiens in their own
  circular orbits.
F. L. Olmsted would certainly
  approve, find it most favorable
  to health and to vigor.
It speaks to me of safeguarding against
  the passage of time, against unhappy
  dispersions of friends.
From the open front door
  the pungent odor of grass
  and the mellow, whispering
  birds mingle with *Prelude and Fugue BWV.*
I always play Bach to encourage
  the garden to grow
  my mind to be still
  my eyes to open
  on a Proustian expansion of tenderness.

# Tracing Jerry

Everyone calls me Jerry.
I am famous as an organizer,
  factotum really, in the
  presentation of food,
  entertainment, and music . . .
The art of the gala.
My assistants, a multitude of inspired
  young people, help me create settings
  that never repeat, stunning to the eyes,
  delicious to the palate, egregious
  to the ears.
It is art to see, listen to, and devour.
As the ephemeral art disappears,
  memories linger and
  people feel friendly and happy.
The kids and I—modesty be damned—
  are exalted. We do it again and again.
I love my job a lot. When not planning
  a feast of some kind, I let my mind race
  over this beautiful, live planet, the
  places I've been, the art I've created.
I thank the Heavenly Lord, the one by
  my side who always inspires me.

## Tracing Jachie

I am Jachie, curator of hair.
In my domain I know I am
  an artist: I cut, I color,
    I sculpt, improvising a lot.
I search for stories under
  the scalps, forgotten styles,
  traces of youth, personal
  faded beauty to be restored.
I love what I do in my
  white and blue parlor,
  huge windows reflecting
  the sky, artwork all over,
  punctuating the walls.
I look at my clients and see them
  as orchids: difficult flowers
  when closed, seductive after
  I open them.
When my soul rejoices in
  its freedom
  I thank the Heavenly Boss,
  the One by my side.

## Tracing Patty

I am Patty the bartender.
I love my job.
It brings me close to the visitors there
  passing through
  drifting in
  greeting me sometimes.
Some sit, some slump.
Some like my looks.
Sometimes they say
  Hey, Patty, you look like
  that lady in *Casablanca!*
  You have the perfect hair!
They tell me jokes
  report who died
  who divorced
  who lost his job.
One lost his right arm far away in the East.
Some stories are bland
Some like a visual jolt.
On my breaks I get out
  scan the parked cars on the street
  studying the drivers.
Is that a lonely Lamborghini down there?
Hell, no, that's just an old Buick,
  well-preserved. Vanity license:
  *Iam Gr8est 34.*
From a distance I see the man
  wearing a T-shirt
  with obscene writings.
He comes close, he offers me
  a lonely pink rose and
  a beautiful friendship.

## Tracing Ania

My name is Ania. I come from Poland.
My job is not just cleaning houses,
   it is restoring order, clarity, fresh air,
   and fresh dispositions all around.
I move fast, dancing to old mazurkas
   in my head.
I am young, beautiful I am told,
   with a personal way of
   presenting myself, master
   of arranging my own objects,
   clothes, shoes, *Vogue* magazines.
I want the eyes to travel from me
   to the space I created.
After work I sit down, let loose my
   long blonde hair, close my eyes,
   thank my Catholic God for my
   husband, my kids, my friends.
I am grateful to the old country
   in my heart and my new one,
   a place with people outgoing,
   hard-working, and generous.

# Tracing Lieutenant Billie E.

I am Lieutenant Billie E, serving my country
   on a very big ship on a faraway ocean.
I am well-liked here, as my natural state
   is serene, respectful, encouraging.
I see only the best in my junior sailors,
   some not even twenty years old.
Smiling at them is not difficult,
   thanks to some wisdom I got
   or got thrust upon me long ago.
Connections spring forth around me
   like many phosphorescent sparks
   like the invisible ones my love, Sara Bella,
   conjures up around me
   unreadable messages
   transcontinentally intense.
Soon I will be with her
   when the sidewalks of my growing-up town
   will sparkle with leaves no longer green
   yellows, browns, and deep bloody purple.
So lovely is this planet Earth
   but I need not thank anyone for it . . .
There is no creator
Only turbulent molecules.
And I am doing my best in keeping it
   peaceful, untroubled, and safe.

## Tracing China P.

I am a quilter from Gee's Bend, Alabama.
My mother, a quilter, raised ten children,
  forever struggling, but made it.
My mother learned me to quilt.
Coming home from school
  we did our chores, then we
  had to quilt til ten o'clock at night.
Did my first quilting as a kid,
  was a star. Still have it.
I am a social worker now.
Love to sing gospel songs, old hymns.
I quilt less but keep my vision clear
  behind my eyes.
My simple vision all my own.
Eccentric improvised vision.

## Tracing Linda L.K.

My name is Linda L.K. I am a painter,
   installation artist, sculptor, inventor of
   images.
In the multifarious art world I inhabit,
   I am respected, even acclaimed.
My work derives from deep thoughts
   and open inquiry . . .
   our precarious existence, the dolorous
   brevity of youth, the lack of compassion
   around the world.
What I create:
   pyramids of amethyst blue shards
   portraits, faces diluted by time,
   a dog on a beach
   sparkling geometry of flowers.
All are commanding entities
   in shapes and colors revealing
   the contours of their immanence.
My brushstrokes are swirling and edging.
I am forever searching and pursuing beauty
   beauty demanded by my vision
   beauty that fills my eyes with tears,
   beauty manifested through evolution and
   chance without assistance of any god.

## Tracing the Reverend

I am the Reverend Kurt C.,
   speaking to you about the Light,
   the uncreated Light,
   substance of the universe
   diffusing into each of us. . . .
White, black, lesbians, gays, and
   the in-between folks.
The Light of God makes no distinction.
 It is total love, perfectly resplendent
   in each of our eternal souls.
We are shreds of his light, created to complete
   his endeavors on this delicate planet.
I am the Reverend K, your spiritual guide.
From the center of my Mandala,
   my dominion of order, will, fate, and love,
   I shall guide you, comfort you, nourish
   your spirit, and excite your mind.
Be blessed, all of you. May you all take time off
   to appreciate the lavender peonies,
   may all of you drive a Tesla
   on your vacation and sing Hallelujah.

# Tracing James L.

James Lester is my name
  known also as Mariner from
  the ancient eponymous poem.
As a newspaperman I focused
  on politicians
  corrupted liars
  buffoons.
Five of my books chronicled
  some powerful crooks'
  unpredicted descent
  into shame.
As I sit in my brown leather chair
  reviewing my life, I, doleful, accept:
  Everyone born has to die under
  heaven, I certainly, yes.
*Vanitas vanitatum*, but I digress.
*Casablanca* is my movie
Pale green my color
The cobalt-blue iris
  that stands erect in
  my mother's porcelain vase
  is my flower forever.
About people, who knows?
They may surprise me one day
The same goes for God.

# Tracing Body

I am Body, accounting is my trade.
I am a mild-mannered, enthusiastic
    man with Nigerian blood in my veins.
Fela Anikolapo is my hero.
Fela, a man from our so-little country
    made himself a superstar, went to
    America.
Singer, composer, leader of a big band,
    played to enraptured audiences
    went home to Nigeria to fight for freedom.
He is long gone now, a Native Son
    who made himself over.
I am a sentimental man.
Reminiscing gives me pleasure:
Here, walking at noon on the avenue,
    checking out the latest fashions,
    super-short shorts, T shirts with
    infernally hot coloration,
    nose rings, latest gym shoes.
I love people, even those who ask me about
    the Lord.
Hey, he is a great artist: this planet,
    those stars, this lake.
I say I am so grateful.
    Sunshine on the sidewalk, wow.
Every night I call on Him: I just called,
    Dear Lord, to say I love you.

# Tracing Hugh

My name is Hugh. I trust that
  I am a lover of words, a crafter
  of sentences vibrant with sadness,
  balanced with quotidian joy.
A poet I trust I may be, Irish poet,
  old, semi-blind, counting my
  steps, testing the air, touching
  the sounds.
So alive in this verdant American park.
Most of my work cannot be
  redeemed, contaminated as it is
  by lust for the rhythms,
  greed for uniqueness.
As things go, when I try again and again
  the right line may appear
  where sincere love is exposed
  on a necklace of words.
That's my contentment, in that
  circular shape, that circular note
  for my God, the Almighty
  to notice and cheer.

# Tracing Steve

I am Steve, retired bus driver
Making the best of my solitude.
I cry not over spilled milk,
   there is a time for work
   and a time for a greater do-nothing . . .
But, O, the noise, the crackling,
   the lamenting, the squirks of my
   Virgil, my companion, my BUS.
What music was there!
   Screeching doors, slamming windows,
   babies undulating, women cursing.
All was cymbals, trumpets, and oboes to me,
   a most unnatural symphony.
Some days I take the train to the city
   find me a secluded corner pavement
   sit down gracefully in a yoga posture
   let my mind disappear.
I grieve not for my past youth
   or the red convertible Jaguar
   I will never own . . .
There is a time to work
   and a time to find a bit of beauty
   and a bit of God, deep, deep
   inside each of us.

# Tracing Francois

I am Francois, creator of spaces private
   and public, uninterrupted lines,
   luminous colors, spareness, fluency.
I was a creator, a doer then.
Now older, I see my creations not so
   important: illusory, destined to fade.
So are my past anxieties with rewards,
   recognition, the fragrance of compliments,
   racing cars and tango dancing . . .
Fading . . . fading . . . all fading away.
This is what I now see: the irrelevance
   and power of existence
   the need to direct our eyes
   to the azure mutable ocean
   to the mysterious dark universe
   to our Planet.
I want to illuminate in my work
   what appears to me as the Message
   from the circular ENSO in my mind:
Our planet is fragile, we must make the best
   of what is before we all disappear
   like golden leaves from a tree
   stirred by wind,
   sprinkled with water drops.

# Tracing Viki

Viki is my name. I inspire and assist
  ladies and gents to look young
  to sustain youth in ways
  both technical and spiritual.
Time is not linear: It can be slowed
  by creative technology,
  research, and innovation.
Take Botox, great for the skin.
Take supplements for an agile brain.
Pilates for the figure, yoga for the spirit.
Then there is beauty, a necessity,
  and art, the essence,
  the center of our perfection,
  the inspiration to remain
  forever young.
I have my own Instruction for a
  prolonged *giovinezza:* Check it out.
Number one: Pay attention.
Number two: Be surprised.
Number three: Work out.
Number four: Drive an electric car.
About God: He is not wearing a
  blue periwinkle toga. I sense him
  as Infinite, invisible, immanent,
  everywhere.
He resides in my heart, fortifies me,
  makes me feel freer
  and more loving.

# Tracing Troy

My name is Troy. I was a short-order cook.
Retired now. Leave alone.
Work a bit fixing up places.
Helping neighbors with their cookouts.
Love the summer heat.
Some mornings I take the bus north to Michigan Avenue.
Sit somewhere around street corners.
Enjoy people walking by.
A lady dressed in white stopped by me asking questions.
   What I like.
   Seasons? Songs? Movies?
I said summer for sure.
I love any song by Ella . . .
Movies, I like where the person
   is a colored man like me,
   proud, good-humored . . .
Movies with no violence. Too much already.
   I am sure the Lord
   will get awfully tired of it.
Sometimes I feel the Lord near me. He listens.
   Lord, I say, come down from the clouds.
   Stop my brothers doing bad things
   to each other.
I can feel his sadness in my bones.
He has no answer.
Very slowly he disappears.

## Tracing Angela

My name is Angela V., ambitious businesswoman.
I infuse my projects with my love of beauty and art.
Art is my moral imperative.
I buy and restore buildings so that art can be displayed,
    enhancing every corner of every room.
I welcome and rent my mini-galleries to clients
    of vision inclined to explore benevolent dealings.
In private life, I am the perfect image
    of omnipotent motherhood.
And of course my kids are beautiful, virtuous,
    and perfectly organized to terrorize me with
    games of unruly imagination.
I move around my diverse daily realities dressed
    to intrigue and stupefy.
I think of myself as a *fashionista*, bringing uncommon
    beauty to the places I visit.
Van Gogh said, "There is no blue without yellow,
    no great deeds without daring."

# Tracing Sharon

My name is Sharon
Proud mother of Ben and Joel
  most industrious, kind,
  hard-working young men.
A retired teacher
I have self-transformed into
  a restaurant manager, secretary,
  chef, welcoming hostess,
  resolving strange calamities
  and bickering in the kitchen.
I have health issues
  some unpleasant neighbors
  but I train my heart to be
  unclouded, self-reliant
  serene over fears
  confident in silent hope.
Going around my historic building
Giving paychecks and compliments to my workers
I fortify myself, humming songs of my youth
"Don't Be Cruel," "Blue Suede Shoes . . . "
At night I often hold conversations with the Lord
  advising him to be patient with us
  (the planet is in a disastrous state)
He changes the subject, tells me to think about
  the hula dance I was a star in once.
Create your own poems, Sharon,
  gently sway your hands and hips to
  "Though this island wonderland
  "She's broken all the *kanes*' hearts . . . "

# Tracing Keith and Gary . . . A Conversation

We are old.
We may be retired.
Who knows?
We hang around Marv's Place most days,
    ordering coffee to last for hours.
I am Keith, he's Gary . . .
I say, Gary, come and see how I magnify
    all the glorious purple martin houses in my yard.
    Those birds, they love me for it.
Keith, stop spoiling those birds.
    Those houses cost a fortune—two, three floors,
    split-level panoramic view of the Ohio River.
    And their pre-dawn singing, it wakes me up
    much too early.
I say, Gary, it is good for you to do some
    early-morning reading to keep your brain
    from being dislocated. All those books
    on politics you pile up like the Tower of Pisa.
Keith, I know my writers, my movies. I get
    political insights, scoops from them.
    What do you get from Harry Potter?
Gary, I get *joie de vivre* from the wizard
    while you get libertarian ruminations.
Keith, it's time to get to Marv's Place,
    disturb those somnolent guys,
    check out the pretty new waitress.
    I heard she is old enough to vote.
Well, Gary, I may be wrong but I doubt it
    when I say, and I quote, voting is forever
    choosing between a totally disastrous
    and a sturdily unpalatable candidate.

# Tracing Jack

My name is Jack, planner of festive events.
I listen, take notes, produce visuals
   of past enticing affairs,
    take suggestions and deliver
    memorable fairy tales.
I give them a mini-reality show.
I admit to delivering on my promises with
   unfussed punctuality, being reliable,
   affable under the direst circumstances.
I am diplomatic, conciliatory, reassuring.
It helps that I compliment the ladies in charge
   a lot . . . I mean a lot.
With my three sons I am the perfect model
   of gentle fatherhood: amiable, kind,
   understanding.
I want them to learn from me to be
   resourceful, optimistic, tenacious.
Tenacity in life is a must.
They must see it in me:
   a loyal, pleasant, tenacious man.

# Tracing Dr. Stephen

I am Dr. Stephen J. G., a dentist
   with an artistic bent.
I create perfect shimmering smiles
   by imagining them first.
I work with devotion and vivacious alacrity
   removing, restoring, reinventing
   smiles to kill for.
My clients like me, confide in me,
   express their fears about the world.
This technological, unfeeling age
   full of tensions and devastations.
I say the world is flux. Evil is seasonal.
It comes with the wind and goes with the rain
   fading away like the last rose of summer.
Honorable people will be crushed sometimes,
   prevail sometimes.
I believe from our present chaos a dancing star
   will be born soon.
She will have a cohort of delicate angels
   dressed like Lady Gaga
   and driving Lamborghinis.
They will make the world and the people
   beautiful again.

# Tracing Sandra

My name is Sandra M.
I am cool and likable.
I work in the design industry,
    analyzing with theoretical rigor
    what sells and what does not,
    what will be selling next.
I must uncover or divine clues in the market,
    harder to predict and less fun than
    watching snowdrops coming up
    from under the snow in late February.
Products like blossoms appear every season
    in tantalizing colors and undiluted promises
    to keep me fresh, self-sufficient, enthusiastic,
    and young.
I am self-directed and endeavor to maintain myself
    in perennial allure and vivacious intelligence.

I can affirm that I am immune
    to pedestrian clothes, movies, books.
All I need is new handbags,
    new evening bags, new shoulder bags,
    small, large, audacious, capricious,
    irresistible.
Bags make me happy, the kind of happiness
    that needs constant upkeep.
More bags, more bags, I am the Don Juan of bags,
    10—50—100—103? . . . Mozart, himself
    a fashionista, knew about the temporary,
    fast-fleeting, sublime happiness of conquest.
Dear Lord, I pray to you, do not induce me into
    more bag temptations.
Gucci, YSL, Jimmy Choo, Prada, Chanel,
    Max Mara, Miu Miu, and all the
    soon-to-be famous.

## Tracing Dustin

My name is Dustin, editor of a very artful magazine.
As a young lawyer, I carried the love of art
  in my marbleized soul.
My refuge, my kingdom, my church was the Art Museum.
In those galleries I learned to select, set my rules,
  choose my territory.
There I ignited my editing and my resolve:
  to intercept and reveal
  the art, the beauty,
  the enthusiasm
  from our clothes, our walls, our plates.
In the magazine I demonstrate how to organize stuff:
How to make it into art, how to appreciate fading colors,
  unrelenting blacks, lace-trembling whites:
I show how to pair for fun the hesitant Monet's *Irises*
  with a turbulent spiked hat or
  how to distend a multi-color dress
  on a chair next to the
  *Rainy Day* of Gailebotte.
I dare the readers to choose:
  *Either be a work of art or wear one.*
This is my job, to edit, contrast, present the best
  as I see it.
"What about the Levante?" my daughter asks.
"Is not that car a feast of excellence?"
She wins. I will write just that before sending
  the new issue of the suburban dreams container
  to every home on the North Shore.

# Tracing Redding

My name is Redding. I am young
  but my thinking is not.
I progressed fast from fairy tales
  to the *Twilight Saga:*
Seeds of comprehension
  sprouting in my brain
  in pale yellow undulation.
I was told I am my mother's work of art.
That is why my steps are like dancing steps
  on a balance beam.
I'll tell you about my mom:
  she sees only beauty
  speaks in temperate voice,
  drives a Levante.
Order, proportion, harmony, style
  on her person and around
  wherever she dwells.
It is my life's intention
  to win her approval
  naturally, in my own ways
  with my own *chocolate fur*
  my red Hawaiian not-too-short shorts . . .
Mom, I will put my arms around your life
  and make my shadow
  shine lovingly around you.

## Tracing Ron

My name is Ron. I own a bicycle shop.
Teach rowing on the side.
The students
  ages nine to eighty-one
  learn to fly in long,
  sleek aluminum shells:
They ask to learn to be perfect.
They practice, persevere,
  anoint themselves,
  stretch their limbs to be harmonious
  with bike wheels and boat oars.
I observe them,
  keeping an existential silence,
  leading without ruling.
I follow in my boat
  absorbing the sound of oars
  slicing water as smoothly
  as geese slice the wind.
A slender rowing line of delicate contours,
  pulsating on the green water of the canal
  shivering beauty under a limpid sky.
I feel a duty to guard
  to sustain the students' flow
  keeping the vision
  the tenderness of efficiency
  that leaves no trace behind.

# Tracing Shelly

I am Shelly, a retired perfume model.
I am very tall.
I hesitate to say I am a presence wherever I appear.
Since a young age, I examined myself
  my bone structure
  my complexion
  my disposition.
What I wear is always a response to my mood.
I walk out of my house flooded in tenderness
  for the people I see
  anxious to like them.
When asked for advice, I say
  study your body
  see what it demands
  invent the image you want to project.
Do not feel inferior and wear drabby clothes
Do not compensate by spending a fortune
  to look alarmingly wrong.
Select a master for inspiration,
  be restrained
  stand tall
  spend less
Train the body to fit the clothes
  that honor your spirit
Love clothes that don't just make you shine,
  that make you glow from the inside.
This is the advice I gave myself
  every lovely day of my long, long life.

# Tracing Peter v. d. G.

My name is Peter v. d. G.
Known to late sleepers as the all-night radio host
   of a small classical station
   from 12 p.m. to 5:58 a.m.
I present, explain, translate selections of eternal
   sonatas, concertos, arias, symphonies.
I talk to my invisible audience
   I gave footnotes, I compare,
   I lighten up even the most revered, imposing
   classical stuff.
I drop little red cherries along
   *Pavans, capricci, divertimenti,*
   dances from the old country
   and from our own bluegrass.
By day I am a baritone classical singer
   most at ease with Haydn's Creations,
   Handel's *Messiah*, the Verdi *Requiem*.
My life is dense with music—
   musical notes, passages, refrains
   float around me incessantly.
*Dell'aurora al tramonto del di.*
I whistle the Kiss of Beethoven like Fritz, my idol.
   or mumble the minuet of the Farewell
   or that of the *La Passione*.
I keep Vivaldi's *Four Seasons* on my cell when
   power-walking with my darling soprano wife.
   Together we step with the *Inverno sopra il ghiaccio*
   in *Primavera col mormorio di fronde e piante*
   *nell Estate con languidezza per il caldo*
   *poi l'Autunno ci insegue con ballo e canti villenelli.*
People tell me I am a star: No such thing for a radio host.
My star is the one who walks and sings with me
   about the love of Robert and Clara
   that impossible *travolgente* love.
Their story so sad it touches the heart of our audience
"This passionate crescendo love.
   Please take it from us
   Make it your own."

# Tracing Frank

My name is Frank.
I am an intelligent, educated older man.
Yesterday I received some questions in the mail
   for a poem to be composed about me.
I typed a SCREAM: make it in plain,
   pedestrian language.
And make it good!
I will tell you I like no poems
   prefer no colors
   abandon most movies
   read about one-half of the books I collect.
This I confess.
I spent my life doing rubber-cement kind of work:
   boring and depressing.
   It made me rich and very well dressed.
I live alone with no agitation
   or illusion about eternal life
   I know better.
About the people of the world, it is sad.
They know not how expendable they are
   how insignificant
   how replaceable
   just like commodities
   they come and they go.
As for myself, I am neither good nor wise.
I accept that my life is fleeting
   as air slowly leaking
   from Michelin tires.
I am left with no desires now
   for all that which I gave up
   all the toys of old age
   all the dead accumulation of stuff
   all this was essential Roman
   *Vanitas, Vanitatis.*

## Tracing Ben

My name is Ben: In wintertime
I am a young contractor
   but when spring distends
   its rosy fingers on the sea
I take my buddies in my
   thirty-foot sailboat
   the slender *Connemara*
Rushing on deep blue waters
   to chase the patterns of the waves.
When fall is in the air
   and the tall trees of my Ohio hills
   are kissed by a tired sun
   we go hunting for rabbits
   fishing for trout
   to cook on open fires
   through the night.
We are young, we get along . . .
I plant white hyacinths
   to celebrate ourselves.
I have reason to rejoice,
   to start a fire,
I want to warm my cold exterior,
   keep an easy smile
   when I wish a good day to
   the strangers up the road.
I am young and won't be for long.
Now is the time for kindness
   making friends a little happier.
It is time for getting wiser:
   This is my daily wish.
   It is the best I can do.

# Tracing Mike

My name is Mike.
In my work as a lawyer
  I collect my facts
  inside Manila envelopes
  to present my cases in court.
Dressed somberly
  curly black hair slick and shiny
  impeccably confident
  I easily win.
I then rush home to my garden of love.
*Guarda guarda il mio giardino . . .*
First I do nothing
  just observe the ripples of grass
  growing freely
  and the attentive flowers
  in quotidian exuberance.
"And so the days flow through my eyes
"But still the days they seem the same."
Soon I move my hands with agitation
  to dig, caress, separate, replant
  giving space and expectation
  to the living miracles I love.
I partake of their lives
I let them expand in aesthetic disdain
  to geometric perfection
I have no moments of boredom
With my plants I am constantly learning
  patience and trust
As they grow jubilant
  my soul is made fresh
  wiser, more cheerfully tranquil
I am at one with the true beauty of nature
  with the poetry of every white little stone.

# Tracing Kurt

My name is Kurt.
I worked as a biochemist until I retired.
I was blessed with a mind attuned to
   mathematics and music:
   the beautiful languages of God.
With joy I devoted myself to understand
   and protect the body and its functions
   while embraced by the opal veil of the music
   of Mozart, Beethoven, and Bach.
I made my life's project to learn
   how cells in our body merge with atoms,
   combine with enzymes and proteins
   to make muscles and bones.
And so we can walk, talk, eat, think, and remember.
When systems or parts of the body break down
   we biochemists, the Magi of our age,
   confront and readjust DNA imperfections
   at the very molecular level.
I was given a glimpse of a world incredibly small
   made of particles fundamentally simple:
They make up our bodies and everything
   we pursue, we desire, we adore:
   our forests, our oceans, our planet.
I salute the elementary particles
   and their elegant dance
I carry them in my heart with all the notes
   of all thirty-two Beethoven sonatas.
I am grateful.
I am content.

# Tracing Jorge

My name is Jorge.
I am a nursing assistant, certified,
   appreciated, I trust, by the patients.
I can listen, I can agree, I show respect.
After work I take my little dogs
   for long walks
   never forgetting their warm coats
   in freezing weather
On weekends I take photographs
   of places and people around me
I give them the images, their memorial
   and they smile.
In early spring when the air is fresh
I go looking for gardens in the shade
   searching for small flowers
   white, pink, yellow . . .
   white, pink, yellow flowers
Memories of Grandma's garden
   white, pink, yellow *mirabilis*
   flowers with a difficult name
I never speak of Grandma now
Grandma's pots of white, pink, yellow
*Mirabilis jalapos*
I take their pictures when I find them
   white, pink, yellow
   little miracles of God:
They live in my cell phone
Grandma lives in my heart
I protect all of them
Never to disappear
Never to let me forget.

## Tracing Beate

My name is Beate.
I founded a gallery to showcase
   the work of rebellious feminists
From a broken-down storefront
   we soon moved to an elegant space
   on a glistening, powerful street.
I was a rebel before this gallery,
   my *Opus Maximus*
   still a rebel many years after.
Seven thousand, and counting, women
   have had a forum here
   all with a William James "will to believe,"
   will to be heard
   will to provoke.
I remember one show
"Home is Where Hell Is"
   tumultuous responses
   insult, indignation, picketing
   also quotes in scholarly papers,
   lectures—and Sales!
My women's gallery has different leaders now
   even more belligerent
   and I keep a watch from a distance.
I read only poetry for real information
   listen only to J.S. Bach when I am
   overwhelmed by
   doubt and resistance.

I make pencil drawings,
   lines and more lines
   and more penciled lines
   different widths
   different moods
They are portraits of thoughts
   delicate or forceful
These are my efforts now
I want to exist as an artist
   maybe even be noticed.

# Tracing Brian G.

*This is the only portrait of a living person not based on an interview with the subject. I read Brian G.'s autobiography and it compelled me to write this poem.*

My name is Brian G.
I wear my hair gell-ified straight up:
  an invitation to wonder.
I am a movie and TV producer
  known universally
  liked, applauded (or not).
I was born afflicted by massive curiosity
  it was my Muse
  it gave me fervor, uninterrupted courage
  like a continuous Locatelli concerto
  in my brain.
I follow my curiosity Muse
  asking questions of people
  deep in particle physics
  science fiction,
  acting, politics, avant-garde art.
I ask total strangers to sit and talk with me
  about their lives, their values,
  dark energy and the end of sex.
I decipher their souls from their choice of shoes.
Now in my middle years
  I am still asking questions
  assisted by my curiosity Muse
  I follow the vertical paths
  of the Ones I must know:
They sit in my vision
  obscuring the rest of the world
  until I take notes.
My *modus vivandi* is my fortunate life.

# Tracing the Circular Painting

My name is Itala.
This is a true story.
I was walking down the street
   in the pouring rain.
A voice said, "I love
   the circular painting
   in your arms.
   It seems to me to be pure poetry
   And I know I have the perfect wall."

"Alas," I said, "This is your painting.
 "Take it."
Kept on walking
   in the steadfast rain
   empty-handed
   Giotto on my mind.

If it keeps on raining it doesn't matter.
The abandoned one
   in the stranger's arm
   is getting paler and paler.
I can feel the sorrow
   In the incessant rain.

# Tracing Itala

The painter's work,
Pale abstractions of
Non-Euclidean geometry,
Hangs bathed in light,
Entities self-invited
Like distant relatives
Consolidated against
The fading of youth.

She said: I wanted people
To forget about food
About the cost of living,
Aging, the visceral
Ingratitude of kids.
I wanted to rescue them
From unnerving banality,
The obsession of shopping,
The terror of death.

I do what I do disregarding
The stock market, the art stars
Their trends and dictates.
I do what I do by building
Erasing caressing . . .
My works are my lovers
I keep them tied to my jeans
Until they can stand
Hermetic and graceful
All by themselves.

I make no plans in advance
Consult no avatars,
The clouds, only the clouds
Let me know when I am done,
When a piece has become
*Quasi una fantasia.*

# Tracing Zacatlán, Mexico

Zacatlán, magical town, your people
Are growers of apples, bakers of bread
Painters of extravagant walls
Your mountains embrace you in
Stately trapezoid drapes kissed by
A very ancient, comforting fog.

Zacatlán, magical town, your streets ascend
And descend in ribbons of pulverized
Stones, surrounded by homes made up
In tantalizing hues, exuberant grays,
Spacious yellows, bloody wild reds,
Astonishing, prosperous greens.

Zacatlán, magical town, your days unfold
In sunshine, rain, and fog over people
Patient, industrious, hard-working, who kiss
Welcoming you with smiles and papayas
Creative people, men in sombreros,
Women in shawls, children with flowers,
They carve, knit, and paint invisible
Fugitive dreams.

# Part Two

# Portraits from the Other Side

# Tracing Paulus Silentiarious

I am still known as Paulus Silentiarious
  alive in *Anno Domini* the sixth century
My surname was derived from my job
  an usher keeping the silence
  in Justinian's palace.
In my free time I would sit on the steps
  of the Hagia Sophia
  and write poems about love
  some not destined for innocent ears,
  realistic poems I would call
  refined in exaltation of some
  pleasures of the flesh.
I had a gift for lyricism: Justinian
  commissioned me to write the *Ecphrasis*
  of his glorious cathedral. I did so
  listing ornaments, mosaics,
  precious stones and marbles
  interminable lists several hundred
  lines long, still a model for
  beginning poets.
For all you living beings who dislike
  getting old, read my lines, see how
  I glorified my lover's wrinkles
  more beautiful than any smooth skin,
  how I would rather bite my old lover's
  pale lips than those of a youth in full bloom
  for I never had a taste for the young.
Now still I would choose autumn over
  a tenuous spring, winter snow over a
  summer sun.

*A.D. 515-580*

# Tracing Calypso

*Inspired by "Six Characters in Search of an Author" by Pirandello, whose imaginary people step out of the pages to be real, I want to give voice to Calypso, a personage from Book 5 of the Odyssey. Homer created her with all the failings and longings of a mortal woman. She is an eternal, even if invented, presence.*

My name is Calypso, a goddess alone by my loom.
Odysseus, my lover, sits on the beach wasting away.
He cries for his distant home, his royal place in Ithaca
   so far away.
For seven years I loved him and cherished him,
   would have made him eternally young as I am.
No way. He got sick of my love, cried to go back,
   to grow old with his wife, who,
   by the way, cannot compare
   in beauty with me.
So it is, ladies. Beauty is useless weighed against
   a life shared, sprinkled with sorrows and joys.
All I could offer him was an eternal strong body,
   blond curly hair, undisturbed musing on sameness.
He was so distracted and bored that I let him abandon me,
   submitting myself to the harshness of Fate.
He sailed off on the raft I helped him make from my trees.
I kissed him adieu with a propitious wind
   to undulate for him the misty waves of the sea.

# Tracing Clotilde

My name is Clotilde. I am a shade
  behind the invisible veil.
From this position I see my home for sale
  with all the collected stuff I cherished:
  leather sofas in blond aquamarine
  crystal languid lamps
  pillows and draperies of lace
  wool hats and Japanese combs
  enviable priceless stuff,
  what earthly fame is made of . . .
Means nothing: I am a shade
  indifferent even to the 1,027 very high heels
  symbol and envy of reflected fame.
Stepping on the inside name of the shoes
  of famous Italian designers used to
  generate tremors of pride on my skin.
  It was a ridiculous thrill.
Storing my vanity in the rainbow-colored heels,
  in the Roman sandals with diamonds and rubies,
  in the boots made of real flowers,
  my vanity in the golden embroidered
  fringed fragile contorted designer shoes.
I am a shade now. I get it. I amassed
  1,027 obstacles to a different kind of life,
  a life I chose not to live.

# Tracing Pierre

I am Pierre T. de C., French philosopher,
  paleontologist, Jesuit.
I studied the universe and saw that it was alive
  with an invisible substance.
I named that stuff divine.
You too are facing this mysterious stuff
  and it buffers you.
Yet you do not call it divine.
Not yet.
Read my book *The Divine Milieu*, listen to me.
The universe is unfolding in a physical evolution
  which I knew also to be a spiritual evolution.
Read all my books, scrutinize them.
Put my theories to the test:
I dare you!
Listen to the glorious silence around you,
  open your eyes, learn to see:
I dare you!
Listen to the glorious silence around you,
  open your eyes, learn to see.
The universe is suffused with divine moving action.
Understand that energy. Its origins are divine.
I call that energy Love.

*1881-1955*

# Tracing Catullus

I am Catullus, poet of the Roman Republic.
   Admired by Caesar, by the people of Rome,
   and lovers of poetry all over the world.
Of my 110 poems, 25 were for you, Lesbia.
   Love of my life. Little did you care
   for me, all you did was laugh . . .
*As the sun doth rise* (still does)
   *it will not do so forever. And when*
   *the light shall fade away, we shall*
   *sleep a never-ending night.*
Lesbia, my dear, no flowers bloomed
   in your heart for me.
O Lesbia . . . restore me with
   a hundred kisses, refresh me with
   another thousand, then give me
   a hundred more. . . .
In vain, in vain, Catullus of the golden voice
   was disparaged, forgotten, without *Pietas.*
   I died young, alone, despised. . . .
Reading my own, now-famous poems
   does not console me. I need a new life.

*84-54 BCE*

# Tracing Eva H.

My name is Eva H. I no longer walk
  in your world as an artist.
   My art, what I created, persists,
   celebrated more and more in
   museums and scholarly books.
In my short life, art was my
  total concern . . . Art as my life,
   irregular, rough, repetitive,
   made of ropes, rubber, latex, and sticks.
"Do not ask what it is,
  rather see what it does."
I was deep in addressing my need
  to find out what I could know
   and trespass from there
   to the unknown quality of Being.
"The art, my life, could be something,
  could be nothing."
Grids, structures, clusters of knitted
  rejected materials . . . I wanted them
   "to say something, say nothing."
My art, my life, was something,
  was nothing:
   a compressed product of my living,
   my rebellion.

*1936-1970*

# Tracing Peter

I am Peter L., a gifted young designer
  alive only till 1999,
  suddenly taken away
  from the world of my parents,
  my wife, Laura, my brother,
  Emery the Great (he called himself
  so at age three).
Emery, dear, I loved you more than myself.
  Still do.
Growing up, I was industrious and calm,
  a self-contained little man,
  happiness seldom with me.
A little artist, spinning colors around
  with amiable vigor,
  tints and blushes
  of exquisite perfection,
  done disregarding all rules
  in a most reckless experimental manner.
I am distant now, but not too far from you,
  Francois, my friend,
  and you, Sandra,
  and you Laura,
  I loved you both.
I love you, Mother, who tried so hard
  to make my brother a lover of poetry
  and flowers, someone who could
  forgive his enemies even if they
  were of his own blood.

# Tracing Lady Emily E.

Even in the assisted living facility,
  I was spoken of as Lady E.
I was distancing, not given to small talk
  or useless dialogue.
I appeared well-dressed, well-groomed, well-spoken.
If I could not understand sentences, I dismissed
  the speaker as uninformed.
I wore rings on many fingers and
  Chanel Number 5 between my thighs.
When my only daughter would visit, empty-handed,
  we spoke little:
I unable to recall, she unable to console.
Suddenly she would part . . .
I pointing my slender finger to the latest issue
  of *Vogue*, my final source of pleasure.

# Tracing D.V.

I am D.V.'s distinguished ghost,
  still alluring when gliding between
  the heavenly shades.
On Earth I was a woman of power,
  style, intelligence, culture—all of it.
I projected a beautifully orchestrated
  and controlled elegance.
On my walks, I illuminated the streets.
What I wrote in the editorial pages of *Vogue*
  raised the consciousness of the American woman.
I investigated, selected, and dictated
  imperious rules of self-presentation
  where intellectual seduction was the aim.
I demonstrated high fashion to be high art
  in the sold-out shows I conceived
  and curated for the Met in New York.
The concept was beauty to wear and beauty demands
  a mind open to knowledge,
  a cultivated mind,
  a mind forever attractive.
I proclaimed there was no need to be born beautiful
  to be wildly attractive.

*1903-1989*

# Tracing Irene

My name is Irene V. I married
   my bright high-school sweetheart
   and cherished him till the end of my life.
I was proud of Charles. Gratitude filled my heart
   for this engaging man with lightning wit.
I was a secretary—slender, quiet, content with myself,
   did my house chores with ease for I saw beauty
   and nobility in simple tasks.
My love for Charles and my three kids was
   undemonstrative but solid:
   I was their island in times of crisis.
   I was a tall tree to rest against.
   I was their supporter, restorer of their confidence.
Undisturbed, I calmed many storms and family
   conflicts.
I could do this for I knew how to stay still in front
   of my God.
A disease left me paralyzed and silent
   but I could still print words.
My last note to my family said:
*Be happy for me. Angels are waiting.*

*1918-1989*

# Tracing Charles T.

My name is Charles. I progressed from
   menial jobs to become principal of a high school in Ohio.
Hard work, determination, voracious reading were gifts
   I cultivated. And, yes, I was blessed with a bright intellect.
I taught my students and my own children
   devotion to learning, generosity, and justice:
   virtues I struggled toward myself, afflicted as I was
   with ambition and consumed by periodic
   melancholic moods.
I enjoyed debates on all topics, as I had an analytical mind
   and a frightening memory.
I could argue about how there is light enough for those
   who wish to see and darkness enough for those of the
   opposite disposition: Pascal agreed with me.
My opinions, ranging from orderly to bizarre, did not
   win me universal love.
Pride, inflexibility, rigid countenance became burdens
   on my soul. It was then that grace my fears relieved.
I prayed on my knees to the Lord to grant me
   a softer heart.

*1918-1998*

# Tracing Calvin

My name is Calvin.
Bachelor, owner of a used bookstore
   when living in your world.
Grew up in an orphanage.
Never had friends or lovers.
I was short, not slender.
Pushed-in face like Socrates
   but without dialectical skills.
I worked years as a porter.
Then I found a very small store
   which I filled with books
   in many languages:
   abandoned books, old, heavy, dusty,
   pages missing or ripped.
I spent hours of enchantment
   staring and chanting words
   I did not understand:
   Latin, Arabic, Hebrew, or Greek.
The stories I imagined
The places I traveled to
The recipes
The advice I guessed
   at how to grow old with some grace.
No girl ever kissed me but I exalted in the
   kisses of Venus.
I had no regrets when I died.
The life imagined, invented, was vastly
   superior to the one I lived.

# Tracing Alex

My name is Alex, born and raised in
  a small town in Illinois.
A pretty girl with no diploma.
I married the son of the butcher
  because the rich boy
  who seduced me would not.
I rewarded my husband with myself,
  a pretty lady looking for fame.
I wrote dime-store lyrics sitting on the bed.
The ugly husband did the shopping,
  the cooking, and the cleaning after work,
  smiling at me all the time.
I wrote dime-store lyrics, pretty words,
  pretty words, lullabyes for my fat shoes:
  pink lipstick and fake eyelashes and a
  colorless heart.
I had no talent: pretty words, pretty words,
  rock and roll songs to whip up lies I told
  myself, irrelevant, signifying nothing.
I died like Sylvia Plath.
I was thirty, a pretty lady with no talent
  looking for fame.

# Tracing Vera L.

I was a seamstress by day
A painter all my free time.
I lived alone with African violets,
   my friends and models lined up
   on grandma's cupboard.
Their language was color,
   brilliant when happy,
   evening-sky pale when melancholy.
Before asking permission to paint any of them
   I would praise, reassure, comfort,
   make them feel loved.
Then we all sang our praises to the Lord.
Only then was I allowed to use
   my self-assured brush
   to make their soul visible.
In my life I never sold an African violet painting.
I heard they fetched high prices
   after I was gone.

*1906-1999*

# Tracing S.M.

I was a *Summus Magister*
  as my best student called me.
I was a sculptor of character.
They loved me . . .
I spoke softly, melodiously,
  telling them how man is
  the measure of everything . . .
To be or to seem to be . . .
Duty and pleasure in
  temporary fusion
*Desiderata* and dichotomy . . .
  most important, endurance.
I was an illuminator of *pensieri,*
  a creator of hypotheses for
  them to delight in.
A decipherer of abstruse propositions
  with jubilant zest.
The students, year after year,
  thousands of them, they loved me.
I was the grand magus, distributor
  of visible words, blue refrains
  charged with soul.

# Tracing Mario W.

My name is Mario W.
Art dealing was my life.
My assistant, Laura, a lady of style
   and of classical bearing
   would alert me when a new voice
   (a minor genius?) arrived
   at the gallery.
I was restless, unsatisfied,
   always on the lookout for
   succulent art, dissonant art,
   art that would describe me.
Art was about me.
I showed what I liked,
   dismissed the rejects
   with ironic alacrity
   oblivious to the pain I inflicted.
I had no friends.
Laura would say my selections
   were portraits of me
   turbulent as my nature
   inevitable, audacious, irregular.
They were to demonstrate a genius
   I did not possess.
From where I dwell now, I cannot bear
   to see the rubbish shown in the gallery
   that used to be mine.
Laura is now a painter in Italy.
And myself
   alone up here
   still with no friends
   still without genius of my own.

# Tracing Phil

My name is Phil, teacher of history
  to privileged, wealthy,
  and distracted children.
I would provoke them to analyze
  and deduce comparisons
  between ancient cultures
  and the one we live in.
I lectured, gave tests, promoted them
  to ventures in our confused world
  to prove themselves.
I lectured and prayed for them
  season after season
  year after year.
I lived with my vigilant wife
  in the suburbs of Boston
  in a small house where we gave each other
  undisturbed love and tranquility.
When cancer took her away
I, a self-contained, contemplative man
  shattered the grey opaque
  Venetian base, a wedding gift
  with deliberate rage.
I retired and sat in my reading chair.
Refusing to eat.
Seneca's *De Brevitate Vitae* my only friend.

## Tracing Lorenzo

My name is Lorenzo.
Mexican immigrant, young and illegal.
I was going to be a great American artist.
I painted with colors sulphuric, emotional, strident:
   dark orange, magenta,
   deep blue, fuchsia,
   furious turquoise.
I painted my Mexican home,
   one room, one door
   and two windows.
The door never closed.
I painted my Mexican home over and over.
I painted the garden, overgrown
   with heavenly flowers.
I painted my Mexican home, nothing else.
Cocaine-infused brushstrokes, all colors
   mixed with my blood.
I was twenty-three when I died.
My canvases, covered in white,
   given to art students for to practice.

# Tracing Aenaes

My names were Aenaes and Silvio.
I dropped the first one—too referential
   to the Trojan hero, exceptionally famous
   then and now with our fiery Romans.
I was somewhat, a bit, famous—potentially,
   quasi-, almost.
I was quasi-famous as the good doctor
   untouched by failures.
They died without my help.
I was quasi-famous for being as good-looking
   as a not-well-known movie star.
I was quasi-famous as a cunningly aspiring
   politician, fit for the Italian regime.
I was quasi-famous as a generous father,
   whenever possible.
As a brother, I was appreciative only in my
   final years.
From where I am now, reviewing my past life,
   I see how unfinished I left it.
How I reached old age in a disaffected,
   inappropriate condition.
I regret having been unprepared,
   unwilling to read all the writings
   on my doors, on my windows,
   on every step of my desolate home.
*Miserere Deo,* even as I do not believe in You.

## Tracing R. K.

I was known as R. K.
A janitor in a rural school.
I was lame, considered less than smart.
Lived with my mother, scorned by kids,
   avoided by neighbors.
Never could I remember dates, facts,
   rules . . . rules of any kind.
Lincoln I loved.
I copied his noble profile
   from the penny over and over.
Never got down my vision of
   his melancholic face.
I was good at cleaning.
Always amazed at how
   the rubbish sparkled
   in the yellow dust pans.
I was slow to learn, but at 23
   I knew suddenly, with clarity,
   before the aneurism killed me:
I knew that I had been searching all my
   life for rules of a most higher order.
God's rules superior to men's.

# Tracing Jerzy

I was very good-looking, a polo player
  of quality, a star writer sought out
  by other star writers.
We applauded each other
  with secret disdain in our hearts.
I wrote novels with ominous references
  to the American media,
  the arbiter of American taste.
They said my voice was like
  nothing else ever.
I knew well why. I extrapolated,
  shook it up, rewrote and
  projected brilliantly
  other writers' words.
No one knew how I did it.
I was a celebrated artist
  impatient, casually cruel.
I traded lies for glittering fame,
  always confusing clamor for admiration.
Walking home one day after a celebrity party
  coke and rum on my breath
  I knew my life had been consumed.
I departed for eternity
  smiling through a plastic bag
  around my head.

*1933-1991*

## Tracing Helen F.

I was an artist who was a woman.
Well-known to a privileged few
I embraced color
Gave form to color
    making it shiver and tremble
    in languorous washes.
I directed color
    under improvised lines
    as joyful as a beautiful message:
    allegro vivace auspicious.
My work demands attention,
    commands to be absorbed.
Help my work to be discovered
    and seen.
Help the glory of my color
    to wake up
    assault and transform
    those somnolent walls.

*1928-2011*

# Tracing the Four-Star Admiral

I was the Chief of Naval Operations.
Highest-ranking officer in the American navy.
I wore a combat decoration I believed I deserved:
It was a mistake.
Inquiries were made
   an interview set up.
I felt circled in, mortified, imprisoned.
The bluish-green ribbon, the V for valor
   snatched away
The texture of my soul
   covered in mud.
I could never face my sailors again.
In the garden by the rose bush
   I pulled the trigger, *Butterfly's* last aria
   drifting from the open windows:
*Must die with honor,*
*He who cannot live with honor any more.*

*1939-1996*

## Tracing Rose

My name is Rose: *La Zitella*
  of a certain age.
I lived alone in a house full of books.
I would clean and dust
  a dictionary in one hand,
  my mind organizing the past
  inventing the future.
I saw myself as diligent, helpful,
  creative, but deserving.
I would take long walks after sunset
  in the park by my house
  I liked the tenebre.
The moon disturbed me with its list
  of hidden interrogations.
I walked alone to find a friend whose
  picture was fixed in my mind:
He would have appropriate qualifications,
  would be courteous, prudent, exacting—
He would hold a long-stemmed white rose
  for me.
I never met him.
I was struck by a speeding car
  on a moonless night.

# Tracing the Cardinal

My name is Bernardin.
I was a Cardinal.
I was not very old
    when sitting in the doctor's office
    a taste of caviar on my tongue
    one of my remaining indulgences
I understood.
Of course, why not me?
Of course it is terminal.
Aggressively terminal.
One last battle?
No, I said, I must go.
I have Christmas cards to write.
    It was August.
I took the service elevator alone.
    Iridescent drops on my face.
My sweat was my acceptance speech
    and a thank-you note to the Lord
    for my redemption.

*1928-1996*

## Tracing Berthe M.

My name is Berthe M., artist from the age of six.
At twenty I was accepted at the Salon de Paris
   and again for many more times.
At thirty-three I was with Pissaro
   in the first of the Impressionist shows
   and in many of the following ones.
And yet my recognition was temperate.
They said mine was feminine art.
Not so! I knew art is not masculine
   Art is not feminine
   Art has no gender
   Art is universal:
For me art was necessary, irreversible.
I dedicated myself to my surroundings
   just as the men did:
Degas painted his ballerinas sometimes without clothes
Monet was stuck on the lilies of his garden again and again.
I did what I saw in my refined social circle:
   the elegant women
   the beautiful children
   the well-tended bucolic lawn.
I was the mirror of their splendor
   their youth, their affluence
   sometimes their frivolity.
I let my brush dance describing only perfection.
I wore myself out every day
   fighting every day to meet my truths
   to explore, expand, improve.
Every single day.
   I wore myself out against rigidity
   against despair
   against failure.

*1841-1895*

# Tracing Harold M.

My name is Harold M.
Electrician by day, creator of cryptic art by night.
My work: small notebooks, one-line poems,
   my name with a famous dead person's name next,
   lists and lists of my name, a famous name, nothing else.
My art, elusive and secret, its beauty for my eyes only.
One day a postcard arrived in the mail
  a picture of an Elvis print
  with a black stamped line: SEND IT BACK.
So I did, I sent it back, signed Harold M. *cum* Plato.
More cards arrived each week, more celebrities,
  more Send It Back.
So I did, Harold M. cum Socrates
  Harold M. with Napoleon
  with Henry VIII
  with Alexander the Great
  back they all went.
The last card arrived on January 13.
The next morning, the paper wrote about a man
  a known but not famous artist, perhaps
  seen jumping from Sag Harbor Bridge
  a probable suicide.
His body was floating on the water
  his hands crossed on his chest
  emerald reflection on his dark wet suit
I knew then he was the invisible sender
His death a large, ephemeral postcard on the waters
  advancing slowly toward eternity.
It was his final work of art.

*?--1998*

# Tracing Christa

My name is Christa L.
I was seventeen when I departed
  for a lighter world in the sky.
I was born with malfunctioning lungs and legs
  and spent my brief life on a shiny wheelchair
  pulled down by gravity.
I was tranquil, never timorous or hesitant.
I was an artist in my mind
  a creator of invisible things
  I had a contented happiness.
Having no visitors at all, I invented
  a retired gentleman to come
  and converse with me.
  He was artistic with a melodious voice.
I said to him, dear sir, take my hand,
  tell me what's there,
  dear sir, do not explain,
  only describe the writing.
Dear miss, he said, I see your life is . . .
Dear sir, I have indeed a limited supply of days remaining
  I have observed the trees changing with the seasons.
  They seem to . . .
Dear sir, the trees only seem to die
  They only go to sleep, to awaken again . . .
Dear sir, I will go to sleep
I will reawaken sometime later
I will marvel again at the peaceful splendor
  of the northern star.

## Tracing Bob

My name is Bob. I lived in the distancing,
   affluent North Shore of Chicago.
My home was a mansion on a leafy street,
   always open to friends, friends of friends,
   people I met on State Street, in Daley Plaza,
   on the train.
My home, the mythical suburban open house.
People approved of me. I was gentle, wise, my
   reputation as a lawyer was eminent.
I spent my free time collecting art from art fairs.
Some was good, most of no value.
I bought what gave me a jolt, what I wished
   I had a small talent to do.
I gave thanks for the feeling of owning
   a beautiful piece, just as I gave thanks
   before every meal.
Here in the land of Thanatos, I am presiding over
   the artwork of talented angels.
 I always knew I was held fast,
   for my Savior loved me.

## Tracing Mary P.

My name is Mary P.
I was sixteen when I overdid it.
I was rejected, cast away, never wanted.
Morning to nightfall
   my mother would sing, go away,
   go away forever
   I never wanted you
   you are so lazy, so dark-skinned,
   so totally inept
   go away, go away.
So I decided to go away.
At first I used my razor ever so lightly
   to impress my living will
   upon my odious dark, dark skin.
Then, deep in the water of my mother's blue tub,
I pushed my razor deep in my chubby wrists.
As the water turned red
I chanted to the Overseer
Dear Invisible Eternal One
   do not let my mother suffer
   not even for a short short time
Let me suffer for her too.

# Tracing Beatrice S. "Tillie"


My name is Beatrice but my nickname was Tillie.
I was a British aeronautical engineer
  and prize-winning racer
  of cars and motorcycles.
As a child, I was convinced
  that both men and women
  could develop great talent.
To become a genius,
  energy and premeditation were needed.
At age fourteen I intended to become one:
  all my time
  my studies
  my practices
  were fixed on one vision:
I will be a prize-winning star in the Royal Air Force.
I succeeded because of lack of distractions
  meticulous attentiveness to all details
  and variations in the field.
There is a great divide between talent and genius.
I crossed that line.
I was never bored
  never confused
  never discouraged
  but prepared and in command.
From my azure, serene location
  my past life seems
  a sustained symphonic *divertissement*
  the modulated whisper of the "Tillie orifice"
  that I invented inside the roaring engines
  was music to me:
More sparkling and delicious than any grand opera
  tenors' impossible high C.

*1909-1990*

# Tracing Maggie S. N.

My name is Maggie S. N.
Sex worker from my vibrant lavender bed.
I was sixteen when he left me.
Melissa, the kid, is almost that age.
A child of the cell phone,
Discontented, angry
Tattooed all over
Unimprovable.

Where are you going, Melissa, my child?
As far as I can, she said.
School she dislikes,
Work she despises . . .

What can I give you, Melissa, my child?
Mother, oh mother, nothing you have
  I would want
  nothing from you I would take.
I am going away as the rain has just started
  taking away my ancient contempt
  for you, mother, this house
  your bed, your face
Such face I don't have . . .
I am walking alone in the rain.
No man will ever admire me.
No one will care if I jump . . .

She left.
She changed, she improved.
I was the one who jumped
  from my window six floors above
  painting the sidewalk
  an embarrassed shade of red.

# Tracing Maestro

I was called Maestro.
Dan is my name.
Maestro pleased me more.
I spent my retiring years at the piano.
Composing gave me total joy.
Waking up, the bedroom still in penumbra,
   I was greeted by musical notes:
   overtures, ballads, preludes,
   intermezzi, duets from my opera,
   songs in a crescendo of furious intensity,
   songs all around me, songs,
   leaves of unsuspected grace, songs,
   echoes of *nobili canzoni,* songs
   tender and cheerful from my distant youth.
I used to take long walks in my faded jeans,
   alone with my songs.
I used to walk briskly, following my musical
   comet, never tiring of pushing and pulling
   my notes, bronze Leaves engraved with my
   markings.
Alluring fragments of new musical compositions
   I was never to write.

# Tracing Jim G.

Jim G. is my name.
I was a self-taught little man
  with elegant manners
  and a vivacious way of speaking.
By the end of my life, I had accumulated
  an enormous amount of classical quotes.
I knew most lines of the *Odyssey,*
  the *Torah*, the *Inferno* (translated, of course).
I was the only one in my vast circle of friends
  to read the *New Yorker* with total devotion,
  recalling each topic for years
When I spoke in big, crowded rooms
  silence prevailed: The grass
  in the garden stood green and erect.
I talked about friendship, grace, mediocrity,
  politics with cheerful abandon.
I read people's souls from the choice of their wives,
  retracing their spiritual progress.
I was a disguised twenty-first century Herodotus.
On the street I had diatribes with innocent strangers.
They had no responses, so I gave them conclusions
  and praised their sharp minds.
I was always in search of psychological truths.
Soon after my arrival up here
  I was told to think of a project of value for
  when I decide to come back to your planet.
How about this?
Exploring Latin as a universal language
  since Esperanto did not work.

# Tracing Bo R. C.

I was eighty when I died
   refusing any technical implement
   to keep me around a few months longer.
My life has been spacious and serene:
   I have been a U.S. Marine
   a master bricklayer
   a race driver
   and a faithful husband.
I did what was required of me
   with grace, finesse, flexibility.
I was always smiling.
I kept myself in harmony with friends,
   the in-laws, the gardeners,
   and the winds of popular approval.
I absorbed the many colors of the sky
   the temperature and moods of the seasons
   the uneven tones of experience
   I carried with me on my departure.
I asked for no funeral or obituaries
   and my ashes to be spread
   on the blue purple waves of Lake Superior
   the evening of the Fourth of July.
I left contented in the knowledge
   that nature has a place where souls
   are purified and renewed
   before coming back.
I cultivated temperance and generosity
   left the planet full of gratitude.

# Tracing Claudia C.

I was the drama and music critic
  of a prominent newspaper
  for over four decades.
"First woman" then,
  and most difficult to please.
My reviews, well written and critical
  procured for me intense dislike
  and unpleasant nicknames.
I could dismantle pretentious
  mediocre work with
  a single stroke of my pen.
My critiques were solid
  based on classical knowledge
  and irrefutable logic.
Plays I approved of
  concerts that delighted me
  were born in perfection:
I would give them my stamp of approval.
I proclaimed: a work of art must be
  genuine, true about life,
  must illuminate, inspire,
  flood our senses with pleasure,
  pain, forgiveness, and friendship . . .
I became famous for being influential.
My columns created and destroyed.
I was listened to.
I never considered writing about me.
If you try to find out who I was
  what I did
  there is little or nothing
  in your oracle Google.
I would like to be rediscovered.
I must tell Them about it.

*1899-1966*

Itala Langmar, a native of Venice, Italy, is a Chicago-area artist, art therapist, and poet. Her artwork has been featured in numerous solo and group shows. Her poetry in English—her second language—has been published in several issues of the Journal of Modern Poetry and in a chapbook, *Regrets and Consolations* (2014). Itala's website is www.artphotonature.wordpress.com.

www.ingramcontent.com/pod-product-compliance
Lightning Source LLC
Chambersburg PA
CBHW021153090426
42740CB00008B/1064